Nothing is what it seems.

AWAKE.

Introduction

When did we as a society become so bat shit crazy? I'm being serious. I recall a time in my life when things were normal. By normal I mean families were husband and wife, maybe a couple kids, family gatherings, summer outings, and church on Sundays. Many refer to these times as "the good ole days". I would have to agree. The leading phrase of "back when" would frequently start a sentence, followed by something that would NEVER happen in today's society. Let me give you an example. My normal was back when someone would mouth off to me, and I could simply close my fist, squeeze it and let off a solid blow to their nose, knocking them off their balance. Many call this "street justice" and call me a redneck, but I still believe in street justice.

The good ole days were back when someone could call you a fagot and you would tell them to go fuck themselves, along with giving the middle finger. Hell, back when you could say "excuse me Ma'am" while trying to pass behind a woman without needing to worry if the person you called ma'am was in fact a woman and not a transexual male, or transexual female. Truth be told, I'm at a loss with all this trans bullshit. Yeah, I said it. Call me a bigot, but the truth is the term "trans" to me refers to

a transmission on a vehicle. Any other "trans" is a mental illness.

As I aged in this life, I've watched many things go right down the shitter. While this is happening, and it's STILL happening, there are three different types of people; The racists/ sexist/bigots, the mentally ill and the rest who are all woke and have no fucking clue what is fact/fiction. If you're reading this and you're thinking *I'm not mentally ill, and I'm not racist, but I do support those who identify as something different than their birth sex* you are woke and clueless. I'm happy to help you see the light- so to speak. Let me explain this layered onion in very simple terms.

In this book I will address several factors that I predicted would happen years ago. Now, I'm a nobody in the sense of predictions. I simply have a solid level of common sense and am a God-fearing Christian man. I read the bible, believe in Jesus Christ and have had a spiritual awakening that has shaken me to the very core. I'll get to all that, but in order to continue on in this book, you must understand, I am not here to sugar coat anything and I will be bringing up topics that are highly controversial and touchy. I have no reservations on calling a spade a spade. If you're ready, let's get started.

Overview

I was born in 1981. I grew up riding bikes, going to the lake with my family and divulging myself into music, lyrics and books. An artist, I designed tattoos for clients and worked as a teacher, prison officer and paralegal, and up until recently, I became a security analyst. Like I said before, I'm not really anybody special.

I was married once before, had a couple kids, but my marriage was highly toxic and that led to a nasty divorce where I was left with nothing but a great level of CPTSD (Complex Post Traumatic Stress Disorder) with NVS & NAS (Narcissistic Victim Syndrome & Narcissistic Abuse Syndrome respectively). It took many years of counseling and specialized testing and therapy to heal from this, while in the process these mental health issues led me down a self-destructive path of addiction and self-sabotage.

I was spiraling out of control, jeopardizing my family, loved ones and new found love with no control. I had hit bottom one day and begged God for help.

I grew up going to a catholic church, was baptized, received communion and was confirmed, but I never really followed God, Jesus or any of that too closely. On this day, I had no one to turn to, so I called out, "Please God help me". I fell apart, crying in the carpeted bedroom of my parents' house while I had no other place to live. My new fiancé held me and it was very matter of fact in what she said. She told me if I really wanted the help, we were going to do this... and this... and this... and she laid it all out on the line for me. With tears falling down my cheeks, I nodded and agreed. I would see an addiction therapist, go to addiction anonymous weekly meetings, get a sponsor, read various books, keep a journal, be transparent about everything, and have complete transparency

with my cell phone at any time. I did it.

Roughly a month or two later, I woke up to go to work and took a breath and realized it tasted purer than I'd ever tasted. It was strange. I felt lighter; like my entire body felt lighter. The sun was extremely bright when I walked outside. I could hear birds chirping that I don't recall hearing before. I was starting to freak out (I know I sound crazy here). I called my sponsor, holding back tears of fear and shared what was going on. He told me to calm down and explained I was having my spiritual awakening. He told me, "Your life will never be the same. You now have the Holy Spirit alive in you once again". Truer words have never been spoken. My life was never the same again and I simply could not go back to the ways I once knew.

I had a purpose now, I had work to do. I was reborn; awake.

Ministry

In February of 2022, I just decided to get ordained as a Christian Minister. I felt a calling and a draw to do it. I'd spent the better part of 6-7 years since my awakening preaching the gospel of Jesus and trying to be a disciple of Christ. I figured why not get ordained? So, I did. Since then, I have always been a member in good standing of the National Association of Christian Ministers.

I haven't taken the Lord's name in vain in 8 years and counting. I have not displayed ANY of my old addictive behaviors in 8 years and counting and although I am still very outspoken and lack the societal filter we're all supposed to have, I am true to the Truth of our Lord and dedicate my life to finding and exposing the absolute truth of the Bible and modern day events that relate to bible prophecy.

Following this path is a lot like the movie, "the Matrix". Keanu Reeves character, Neo, was given the option of taking a red pill, which would enable him to understand what was actually occurring outside the illusion created by the Matrix, or a blue pill, which would allow him to return to experiencing only that illusion. Once you make the decision to take a certain pill; that's that, and you cannot return to make another choice.

In this scenario, asking for God's help, being reborn and the drive to find the truth of this life, I have taken the "red pill". No matter how much I try, I cannot unsee the things I've seen and cannot turn away from what's really going on in this matrix of a world. I will show you more of the exposure as these pages turn.

The Matrix

Perhaps you've heard the world being referred to as "the matrix". This is both comical and factual. It's an oddly unbalanced balance between fact and fiction. When you watch the news, read the paper, hell, even stand outside in your grass and look up, is this actually what is going on or are we living in a simulation? Alright, alright, by now, most people are laughing at me simply because the concept of us all living in an illusion is outside our conscious comprehension. We just can't wrap our head around it, which is why it IS so possible.

Go outside and look up. Are those clouds in the sky, or chemical trails (also known as Stratospheric Geo-Engineering) sprayed there by some branch of our government to control weather patterns? I know, this sounds like something out of a science fiction movie, but unfortunately for us, this IS our reality. I have read about this and watched several interviews with pilots being given the order to release chemicals into our skies at various altitudes. They are paid $20 per gallon of chemical released. The contents of the chemicals are primarily aluminum, barium and strontium, and other materials such as arsenic, titanium and thorium.

These chemicals alter barometric pressure and filter the sun's UV rays to both control the weather in certain parts of the country. This can cause drought, flooding, crop control and ecosystem control. Illnesses and deaths have been linked directly to chemtrail spraying and are numerous and varied, including a horrific disease called Morgellons. The National Institute of Health (.gov) has a great article and explanation of this disease. These chemicals are in the air you breathe, the water you drink and the soil your food is grown in. Birds are falling dead out of the sky; trees and crops are dying, and so are we.

Much of this was once a conspiracy theory, but now it's been silently made public. You can find anything you want to on this subject. The United States used this tactic while in Vietnam for the Vietnam War. They sprayed Chemicals (aka "chemtrails) which caused relentless rain, flooding and would then cause the Vietcong to struggle in their fighting, ultimately losing the war. Now, they're using these same tactics on American soil.

Turn on the television and watch the evening news. Try channel 11, then 9, then 5, 4, and so on; or whatever local news channel you have in your area. I promise you each one shares the same story, and avoids the same story. Why? Propaganda. Agenda. Narrative. The mainstream media is ruled by the US government and they will report only on what the shareholders say and how the shareholders tell them to. Not often are there "feel good stories". More often it's war, crime, COVID, CDC, FDA, etc. They're reporting certain stories in a certain way to enslave us into fear. This is why they call tv shows "programs". They're slowly and methodically programming the population to comply with their narrative.

Remember the COVID19 Pandemic? You couldn't turn on a TV or read a newspaper without seeing global panic, masks, biohazard suits, needles, the images of biohazard and FDA, CDC, specialists and doctors advising staying home, wear a mask, get the vaccine.... This was all scare tactics and when shown all over the globe, it became a global fear. All of this mask wearing, economy shut down, people hoarding toilet paper and canned goods like it was the apocalypse over a virus that was man-made and had a 4-6% death rate. Meaning of the entire world's population, only 4-6% ended up dying from COVID 19. This was one of the most curable diseases we've ever seen.

The basic flu virus that hits nearly everyone every year of their lives is far more deadly than the Coronavirus, yet we placed our trust in the CDC and FDA to take care of us. We believed what they told us. If they told us we were going to die if we didn't wear a mask, we panicked and wore the damn mask.

How many of you readers wore the approved COVID19 prevention KN95 masks? According to these "experts" wearing the KN95 mask was the ONLY way to truly prevent COVID19 from being contracted. During the time of mass chaos, I saw thousands with a painter's mask from Home Depot, or a cotton hand-made mask, or even a handkerchief tied around their neck. Apparently, that was acceptable. Did anybody else laugh their ass off at this complete clown show? On one hand you have these extremely high up medical professionals working for the Center for

Disease Control and Food and Drug Administration along with the Department of Health coming together to announce the scariest virus in the world's history with (at the time) no vaccination for it. They're telling us to do this or that, or avoid this or that and we will be safe, yet thousands did not comply, and were just fine.

Let's chat about the vaccine a bit, shall we? The US Government shelled out $30 Billion dollars for the COVID vaccine. Ok, that's a lot, but here's what gets me. According to the CDC, it takes on average 5 to 10 years, and sometimes longer, to assess whether the vaccine is safe and efficacious in clinical trials, complete the regulatory approval processes, and manufacture sufficient quantities of vaccine doses for widespread distribution. So, can you explain how COVID19 was essentially introduced in November 2019, and in December of 2020 worldwide vaccinations were being conducted?

Yeah, neither can I. According to fda.gov, it does not state that the COVID vaccines were approved by the FDA, but it does say they were "released for emergency use".

So, they couldn't approve the use but gave the go-ahead anyway? Hmm… I will tell you there is quite the rabbit hole here. Care to fall down it? Let's go back a little bit.

As a Minister, I study theology; or the studying of the bible and God. In the book of Revelation, which displays the end of times for mankind, it talks about a choice that is going to be made. A choice each human being will have to make. To follow Satan and be cast to hell for eternity, or follow God and spend eternity in heaven. This choice will come down to a simple decision. To accept, what is written as "the mark of the beast" which will be on the right hand or on the forehead. So, there's a couple things here, and we will circle back around on this, but for how, the vaccine was NOT the mark of the beast as many feared. The vaccine, or "jab" was given in the shoulder.

However, in order to deceive the people into following satanic ways, they need to condition us to follow the masses. First it was mask mandates. Either wear a mask or you can't do this or that... Next it was the jab. Either you get vaccinated and carry the card or you can't fly, travel, or work at many places. It's a ploy to force people into complacency and confirmation. The concept of "don't think, just do as we say". Now we're seeing perfectly healthy people suddenly falling dead for "no reason".

Everything happens for a reason. I found it interesting how when more and more athletes, and others are dropping dead randomly, the FDA and CDC were the first to address the issue stating that this was not related to the vaccines, or boosters or variant vaccines. Yeah, variants... COVID, Delta, Omicron...

Covid started it, they tried modifying Covid into Delta to control more of the population, but it didn't really take, so they threw out Omicron.

Omicron is an anagram for Moronic. Yeah, they hid it in plain sight. They think we're morons, but we are because we keep falling for their bullshit.

Pride

I don't care if you're gay, or lesbian or even bisexual. That makes sense to me. I'm not saying the Bible supports it, because it doesn't. People say, "I was born this way". I do not disagree. But this is why Jesus says, "You need to be reborn". What doesn't is this completely fucked up pride "LGBTQA+". I mean, seriously. How many other letters do you all need to add? And the plus sign? What's that for? Did you know that in 2023, when I'm writing this, according to sexualdiversity.org, there are officially 107 recognized genders in the world? That's ONE HUNDRED AND SEVEN. Remember when I talked about "back in the day"? Yeah, back in the day, there were two. Male and female.

Well, let's call it like it is. Even today in 2023, there are STILL two genders. Male and female. There are so many documentaries out there that talk about how some women have penises and some men have vaginas. Come the fuck on! No. That's all part of the mental illness circle. In the 1990 movie "Kindergarten Cop" with Arnold Schwarzenegger, there's the scene where a little kid comes up to Arnold and says, "Boys have a penis, girls have a vagina". Even that kindergartener knew that!

If we go down the scientific rabbit hole, we can see that each human being has DNA strands that make up their biological existence. Within that DNA each person has two chromosomes; either an XX or an XY. Depending on what chromosome you have, determines whether you're a male or female. So, you can take your 107 genders and shove them up your fluid-sexual asses. It's all garbage and propaganda. There are officially TWO genders; Male and Female. If you don't like that, I'm sorry, but this is the truth. If you are a female and feel like a man, you don't need a sex change, you need a good therapist. Simply put.

While we're on the topic, men cannot have babies. I know there are many who would disagree with me, but the fact still remains, women have children, men have sperm to impregnate the woman. Biology. Now, I read an article where a female who identified as trans, and as a gay male, had a boyfriend who got them pregnant. This is not confusing; they're just a female who got pregnant. Nothing more. Stop the nonsense. This is a mental health issue and needs certain attention. It does NOT need the attention of a medical professional to pump you full of hormones or hormone blockers, surgeries or the support of a mental health illness pride group. Let's get back to simplicity and basic common sense.

With these 107 genders, there are well over 47 different sexualities in 2023. Sexualities, meaning, for example, gay, lesbian, bisexual, demisexual, and the list goes on. The difference is explained as sexual identity is who you love, whereas gender is who you are. Explained by sexualdiversity.org, a liberal platform for promoting inclusiveness to those who find they don't fit into a certain "social group". Again, nonsense. It's becoming, or already is a reality that those of us who are born male/female and are heterosexual (straight) are a major minority in today's society. We are now finding ourselves not fitting in, so this begs the question. Should I, as a straight male, surgically alter myself to match another person so that I fit in better? Should I start taking hormones or hormone blockers so I fit in better? Maybe I should consider slicing my penis to make a vagina and join the trans movement so I fit in better. I'm hoping you can sense my sarcasm with this. The truth is, I will not be doing any of this nonsense, because it's not who I am. I am a man who likes women. I do not use pronouns either. Simple enough. Because I now fit into a minority, it does not change who I am nor does it make me want to fit in. If I was the only one left, I would be my own social group. Those who have no solidity in who they are, are lost, scared and unsure of themselves and the life they're in. That's a scary place to be and the best treatment for that is therapy.

I watched a documentary the other day by Matt Walsh entitled, "What is a woman?" The entire hour and a half, he went around the world asking everyone from women's rights activists to highly trained medical and psychological professionals what a woman is. Surprisingly and slightly comically, no one could answer that

question. He even simplified the question to those interviewed by asking, "Am I a woman?" without laughing. Even then, some couldn't answer that. Some answered, "You could be. Do *you* think you're a woman?" He was baffled. One of the biggest takeaways from this film was of all the places he went around the globe; America was the ONLY place this absurdity is happening. Every other country, large or small, all knew what a woman was, what their role was in their society and why a man isn't a woman and vice versa. America was the only country that was clinically confused. I even lost my words when they interviewed a group of women who were stating they were actively trying to remove the term "woman" from our language and replace it with "Birthing people" to include the trans community. Seriously? Along with this was the movement to change "Mother's Day" to "Birthing people day" and "Father's Day" to... well, God only knows. It's no surprise we're self-imploding as a country. We have a vegetable for a President who literally is a puppet for the World Economic Forum, who we will discuss later, but is the one single entity

that controls everything in this world. They say
jump, our

president asks, "how high?" then falls up a set
of stairs. OMG (facepalm).

One World

Biblically prophesied, in the end of times, we will see a one world government, one world currency, one world religion and one world leader. Sounds far-fetched, but what if I told you we were already over half way there? In 2019, the Muslim, Christians and Jewish communities all combined together to build a third temple which again, was prophesied in the bible within the book of Revelation. The joint declaration, titled "A Document on Human Fraternity for World Peace and Living Together," was signed by Pope Francis and Sheikh Ahmad el-Tayeb, a grand imam of Sunni Muslims, during a visit by the pope to the United Arab Emirates in early February 2019. The headquarters has been named The Abrahamic Family House and was built on an island in the middle eastern city of Abu Dhabi. One thing that was made clear in this document was Abu

Dhabi is a part of the United Arab Emirates (UAE) where it is illegal for Christians to proselytize and conversion from Islam is prohibited. The Pope represents Roman Catholicism where Christians are free to convert to Islam, but citizens of Abu Dhabi are not free to choose Christ. *What?!* My thoughts exactly.

The One World Religion Headquarters has three buildings; one building each representing the mosque, church, and synagogue. However, the church is not permitted to have a cross on the building as a method of identifying it, as it is illegal to display a Christian cross on a building in the UAE. Stay with me here... Teaching that Jesus is the only God is considered to be an act of insulting Allah or the Prophet Muhammad and offenders can be subject to imprisonment for five or more years, fined from 250,000 dirhams ($68,100) to two million dirhams ($545,000), and Christians may be deported.

Dirhams being the main currency (at the moment) of the United Arab Emirates.

To add to the confusion of bringing understanding and tolerance, Sunni Muslim leader, Sheikh Ahmen al-Tayeb, who is widely described as a 'moderate' Muslim, strongly believes that Muslims who convert from Islam to any other religion (including Christianity) should be killed. So, the idea of the One World Religion Headquarters is to bring tolerance and understanding, then why build it in a Muslim country where conversion is illegal and why do it together with a Muslim cleric who teaches that Muslim apostates should be killed?

Isn't that the opposite of tolerance and understanding? More nonsense. Nonetheless, every major change always comes in waves. This being the first wave of the book of Revelation, the second being one world currency.

According to the United States Federal Reserve, the world has "begun implementation to run on one currency – and you will need an identification chip in order to use it. Everyone will be assigned an identification chip at birth, and this will be our new form of identification and currency. You will not be able to purchase or sell anything without this chip implant. This chip will make it more secure and convenient to purchase things in the future. Life will be easier but we will lose our sense of privacy." Now that I've quoted a line within the Federal Reserve official website, I will quote the bible in the book of Revelation. Revelation 13:17 states, "and he provides that no one will be able to buy or to sell, except the one who has the mark, either the name of the beast or the number of his name." "Beast" is referring to the devil, or Satan, the god of this/our earthly world. Re-read this paragraph. Did you notice the mirroring of language? As they say, the devil is in the details.

Previously in this book, I said I would address this issue later, well, it's later. The Federal Reserve mentioned being assigned a chip at birth, meaning newborns will have this microchip, which is about the size of a grain of rice implanted in their right hand between their thumb and pointer finger. Since 2020, this microchip has been implanted in the hands of thousands around the world to prepare for the one world currency, which has been announced to be Bitcoin. At least to begin with, eventually Bitcoin or Blockchain, will transition into FedNow. Every element of finances will be digital, and the retirement of the United States Dollar will occur between 2023 and 2024. The dollar will be useless and only those who have a bitcoin account AND the microchip will be able to buy or sell.

So, what happens if you refuse the microchip (mark of the beast)? The one world government (World Economic Forum now) will force you to take it or be imprisoned or be killed for refusal to comply. This decision will be yours to make when it comes down to the line. What will you choose? You will be able to push it off and push it off, but they will eventually come for you. This is not to scare you, but to prepare you. What will you do? What if your spouse is scared and agrees to accept the mark? The book of Revelation continues on with chapter 14, verse 9-10 regarding the "what if's" saying, "If anyone worships the beast and his image, and receives a mark on his forehead or on his hand,

he also will drink of the wine of the wrath of God, which is mixed in full strength in the cup of His anger; and he will be tormented with fire and brimstone in the presence of the holy angels and in the presence of the Lamb." What does this mean? It means if you accept the devil's mark (microchip) you have chosen to ignore God and the path to heaven and will be cast to hell for eternity while the angels of heaven along with Jesus Christ watch.   Pretty intense.

Have you looked at the back of a one-dollar bill? I mean *really* look at it? On the left side, surrounding the pyramid with the eye are some Latin phrases:

- Novus Ordo Seclorum = "New World Order"
- Annuit Coeptis = "He nodded as he began"

Why would it clearly state New World Order and the phrase about nodding as he began? The book of Revelation does talk about the New World Order.

In April of 2023, President Biden signed an Executive Order approving the transition of the dollar (paper currency) into a fully digital one; Bitcoin. (Look it up; it's on Whitehouse.gov) Worldwide, all countries are doing the same with their current currency. Once all transition to their digital currency, what's called, "FedNow" will be implemented worldwide as a One World Currency; also written in Revelation's Prophecy.

FedNow is the way for the government to have full control over everyone's spending. In basic terms, you will not be able to buy or sell ANYTHING "under the carpet" anymore. EVERYTHING will be documented and tracked. FedNow will be promoted as a SMART app, and you know what SMART is an acronym for, right? Stay tuned...

Parallel to the OWC, and already started in Sweden in 2022, is the implantation of the microchip that they're placing on the right hand between the pointer finger and thumb (Revelation's Mark of the Beast).

It will be mandatory to accept the microchip. If you do, you will have access to EVERYTHING that is you. Your finances, security, employment data, financial data, ability to lock/unlock your home, purchase goods, and the list goes on, BUT you will also have sold your soul to the devil.

If you decline the implant, you will face corporate and societal rejection. You will not be able to purchase ANYTHING, or make any payments, or even access your finances from your employer. You will end up very quickly losing your entire life, BUT you will have saved your soul.

So. Take some time to think this over. You will be faced with a choice, to live a great Earthly life, but face eternal damnation, or starve, be homeless (live off nature in hiding) but live forever in Heaven.

Not just words in a book. Prophecies that have come true and are currently unfolding right before our eyes. This will happen. It's just a matter of time; Oh, and when the dollar is transitioned, it will not be slow and gradual, Theologians and experts suggest it will happen overnight. You will wake up and unless you're using Bitcoin and have had all your assets turned over to Bitcoin, you will not have access to any of your finances. Call me a conspiracy theorist now, call me correct later.

This. All of this is literally knocking at your door right now. It's here, it's coming soon; quickly. This is the time to really sit down and consider this situation. I have thought about it and for what it's worth, here's my decision. Fuck you. Yeah, that's right. I will not accept the mark, no matter what. One of two things will happen to me. Either I will be taken, imprisoned, tortured, and left for dead, where I will spend every waking moment praying to God and following His ways, or I will pay close attention to what they're coming for me and get outta Dodge (as they say). I will find a large forest and live off the grid as a hermit in the middle of nowhere, surviving on whatever, I can, however I can, until Jesus comes to bring me home. Neither decision is convenient nor pleasant, however neither decision leaves me spending eternity in the burning hell that is pure torment. I am planning on spending eternity in heaven with my Lord and savior Jesus Christ. Nothing will make me falter. I just pray and hope my spouse and children follow my lead and not cave. This is a worry, and one of the very few I have these days.

In September, 2010, from the Office of the Director of National Intelligence, came a quite lengthy document entitled, "Global Governance 2025: At a Critical Juncture". There's fine print at the bottom that reads, "Inquiries regarding this report may be made to Mathew Burrows, Counselor to the National Intelligence Council, on (703) 482-0741 and to the EU Institute of Security Studies on 0033-1-56-89-19-51."

In this document, several entries were made relevant such as, "The Global Governance 2025 project is innovative in many respects. This is the first time the NIC has jointly developed and produced an unclassified report with a non-US body. Global Governance 2025 provides an important step with a view to future joint projects on matters of common interest." Common interest? Please explain!

Let's start here. Have you ever heard of a man named Klaus Schwab? Probably not. Here's why. Klaus Schwab is the CEO and founder of the World Economic Forum, established in 1971. Annual meetings take place in an isolated and remote location in the Swiss Alps. It's said that "People who cannot be

seen together in public meet here". Schwab's father, Eugen, a Nazi confidant and industrialist of Adolf Hitler, was a major role model for his son Klaus. When Klaus formed the WEF, the intention was to organize, and implement orders for world leaders who would meet annually. He provided major funding for world leaders to act on his orders. Essentially, HE is the world leader. In 1971 when the WEF was formed, he provided billions of dollars for world leaders, celebrities, and religious leaders to act as his puppets and spread his agenda worldwide for long-term conditioning of the human race. Like how the Nazi's controlled and conditioned the Jews in WW2. He took and is taking the
same concepts and using today's modern technology (phones, electronics, tv programs, social media, etc) to herd the human race towards full and total compliance of what's to come in the near future.

So, in actively digging and falling down the rabbit hole of Mr. Schwab's activity, I've found that one of the elites that partakes in his annual meetings among presidents, celebrities and other world leaders was none other than a Dr. Anthony Fauci. Weird, right? If you recall the explosion of COVID and the global pandemic, Klaus Schwab was the one who ordered the implementation of the non-FDA approved vaccines, mandates, shut downs, consequences for violations and non-compliances and the related. He was quoted as saying, "For the success of our program, societal groups must be conditioned to expect less and rely more on authoritative entities." So, if I'm understanding this correctly, the main head honcho is saying he wants to make us as people conditioned to be used to expecting less in life and relying more on our government. This is not at all what the Constitution of the United States says.

Klaus Schwab, in fact, published a book in 2010 entitled, "The Great Reset: A Solution to the World's Problems" in which there is some hinting or alluding to the need for a global pandemic that would control the world's population, while instilling a common fear to gain control and behaviors of people. He then released "The Great Reset Initiative" which is a direct reflection of how to use the COVID 19 pandemic to transition into a "community" government, also known as a one-world government. Not surprising, some of the most supportive members of Klaus Schwab are Political leaders such as Canadian Prime Minister Justin Trudeau, U.S. President Joe Biden and former New Zealand Prime Minister Jacinda Ardern. They have endorsed the idea of "building back better", as has former UK Prime Minister Boris Johnson, not to mention many A list celebrities such as Leonardo DiCaprio, Tom Hanks, Julia Roberts and the list goes on.

So, I've outlined the one-world this and that that is already being activated, so what does this all mean? Why is it important to know and understand at this time? Let me lay it out for you. There's an outstanding documentary created by Mikki Willis called, "The Great Awakening". It's being removed almost as fast as it's being posted online. I would highly advise watching it. Regardless, there was an interview with a Chinese woman who moved to the United States as a child and became a citizen that really summed it all up. She became emotional talking about how in China, they ran a communist government and what it was like living like that.

She went on to explain how she came to America for the "American Dream", which was freedom and future. She began crying saying that each day, America is becoming closer and closer to being a communist country with our president and social agendas. She said something that really hit hard. Crying, she said, "I'm scared because when and if America becomes a communist country, I have nowhere else to go." Can you imagine what it must be like for her? Sharing memories of people screaming and being imprisoned by law enforcement for non-compliance of their government rulings. Rulings as simple as when they tell their citizens not to spend this or that ON this or that, and they do, they go to jail or are fined thousands. There is no freedom in a communist country.

We are America, our founding fathers based the entire Constitution to hold the government accountable BY the people for the best interest OF the people, not the other way around. The Constitution was based on Life, Liberty and the Pursuit of Happiness. In 2023, our life is being monitored, controlled and manipulated, and/or liberty is being taken away and where is the pursuit of happiness anymore? Look around. It's very difficult to find happiness in a country or a world that is falling apart. In this chapter we will get into the meat and potatoes of the Constitution, which is different from the Declaration of Independence. If you aren't sure of the differences, simply put, The Declaration of Independence, which officially broke all political ties between the American colonies and Great Britain, set forth the ideas and principles behind a just and fair government, and the Constitution outlined how this government would function.

Many highly ranked specialists, psychologists, and scientists have agreed on a commonality amongst the organized chaos that is the United States. This agreement is based upon the war that they are silently waging on the American people, and quite honestly the people around the world. It is a war by division. Division of the people. The old adage says, "Strength in numbers", so if they break down those numbers, the obvious result is us as people lose our strength and lose the war. This is exactly what's happening within American society right now. The segregation between Democrats and Republicans, or Liberals and Conservatives has left a wedge. The segregation between straight people and those who fall under the LGBTQIA+ community are massively segregated. Quite honestly, the origin of the phrase, "We the People" was established in 1787 and was stated as, "We the people of the United States, in order to form a more perfect union, establish justice, insure domestic tranquility, provide for the common defense, promote the general welfare, and secure the blessings of liberty to ourselves and our posterity, do ordain and establish this constitution for the United States of America." That one line in there saying *Secure the blessings of liberty* has been thrown to the wayside. The entire Constitution of the United States was based on FOR the people, BY the people. Who is "people"? You are. I am. This guy over here is. We all are the people. The foundation of the Constitution was that we as a society are in charge of our government. Somewhere along the way, those lines got blurred and now we the people are like mice in a maze, with those in lab coats (government) controlling where we go, what we eat and documenting the results. It's sickening.

Let's take a closer look at the actual importance of the Constitution, shall we? The Constitution is founded on seven basic principles: popular sovereignty, limited government, separation of powers, federalism, checks and balances, republicanism, and individual rights. Popular Sovereignty, simply put, is basically saying that **all political power is vested in and derived from the people**. All government of right originates with the people, is founded upon their will only, and is instituted solely for the good of the whole. What a powerful language they used, and used deliberately to avoid what is happening right now in 2023. Limited Government states that government officials cannot act arbitrarily when they make and enforce laws and enact other public decisions. Government officials cannot simply do as they please. Did you hear that? They cannot simply do as they please. Ok, moving on. Separation of powers speaks of the three different branches of government; the legislative branch (makes the law), the executive branch (enforces the law), and the judicial branch (interprets the law). No one branch can have control by themselves. Federalism is defined as the sharing of power between national and state governments. Blanketly speaking,

checks and balances is to ensure that no one branch holds too much power, which piggybacks on both Federalism and separation of powers. See, they really intertwined the language to leave no room for 'gray areas. They were deliberate in their vision. Republicanism is a theory of government that emphasizes the participation of citizens for the **common good of the community**. The responsibilities and duties of citizens are paramount, and the exemplary citizen readily subordinates personal to public

interests. Again, WE THE PEOPLE. Lastly, individual rights refer to the ability to express ideas through speech and the press, to assemble or gather with a group to protest or for other reasons, and to ask the government to fix problems. It also protects the right to religious beliefs and practices. Also known as the First Amendment right.

First Amendment....... Fundamental Freedoms

Second Amendment......Right to Bear Arms

Third Amendment...... Quartering Soldiers

Fourth Amendment.......Searches and Seizures

Fifth Amendment..........Rights of Persons

Sixth Amendment... Rights in Criminal Prosecutions

Seventh Amendment.... . Civil Trial Rights

Eighth Amendment......Cruel and Unusual Punishment

Ninth Amendment......Unenumerated Rights

Tenth Amendment.......Rights Reserved to the State & the People

Eleventh Amendment....Suits Against States

Twelfth Amendment......Election of President

Thirteenth Amendment.....Abolition of Slavery

Twenty-Sixth Amendment....Reduction of Voting Age

Twenty-Seventh Amendment......Congressional Compensation

Now, many of these we as everyday Americans tend to forget about, or aren't as important as others depending on our everyday lives. Having said that, there are a few that you as an everyday American should really know. The First Amendment is your basic freedom of speech. This governs and protects freedom of speech, the press, assembly, and the right to petition the Government for a redress of grievances. This is what America is and was based on. Freedom. As each day passes, you should be able to tell that there is a very subtle breakdown and dehumanization happening to us where our First Amendment rights are being poked and picked at without us even realizing it.

Look at social media as one example. If you post something that can be deemed as offensive or "hate speech" your post is removed and you are not able to use that platform for a selected period of time. If you publicly voice your opinion, you could very easily face jail time for being unruly or "enticing a riot". You have to be careful of what you say, and more importantly, how you say it. Like I mentioned earlier in this book, they are slowly and methodically censoring and controlling us without us even realizing it.

The Second Amendment is a very popular one in America. The Right to Bear Arms. This is also a very controversial subject as many feel that this Amendment was implemented in the 1700's where you had to have that muzzleloader ready to shoot when someone wanted to infringe on your land. Yes, true, however, even today, in 2023, I question how many people have their conceal and carry permit? How many people carry a loaded 9mm or 10mm on their hip for their protection? Protection from what you ask?

Evil. Crime. These days it's almost like you NEED to be packing heat to stay alive. Many cities have an insane crime rate and people are robbing or assaulting others in broad daylight while they chant "Defund the Police!" The 1700's were a lot like the Wild West of the 1800's and the 1800's were a lot like today's communities. I'm not in any way saying everyone should be carrying a loaded gun, or even a fully automatic assault weapon, but honestly, if a person wants to, that's their American right to do so. This right was stated in 1787, and is still enforced today. The biggest issue with the concept of one-world currency and having everything digital is the purchase of firearms and ammunition. Theoretically, if the ability to track purchases is implemented, the algorithm they will implement will monitor and track purchases of guns and ammo. If they feel you already have "too many" of one or the other, they will simply decline the purchase, and you will not be able to purchase. Yeah, it really is that simple. They will conveniently ignore the Constitutional language on limited government. An honest and real question is when they do, who will argue it? You? Then under their new one world government, you face imprisonment. See how this is all connected? Moving on.

The Fourth Amendment prevents unlawful searches and seizures of persons and/or personal property. Meaning, for example, if the government wants to take your guns from you because they feel you're a threat to National Security (it'll happen), they cannot simply walk in and take them. They MUST have just cause along with a search warrant or court approval. Again, be prepared as they will find a way around this one too.

The Fifth Amendment breaks down into five rights or protections: the right to a jury trial when you're charged with a crime, protection against double jeopardy, protection against self-incrimination, the right to a fair trial, and protection against the taking of property by the government without compensation. Again, many, if not all the Amendments of the Constitution are intertwined with each other to ensure justice is followed, and we the people aren't taken advantage of.

The Eighth Amendment is another important one you're going to want to remember. A part of the Bill of Rights, this Amendment was designed to protect criminals from excessive punishment. It forbids the government from using torture as well as excessive fines and bail to punish people who have broken the law. Meaning, if you're found in violation of anything the government feels you've done to wrong them, they cannot punish you excessively for the "crime" you've allegedly committed. It doesn't mean they won't punish you excessively, it just means you have rights that prevent that.

All of the Constitution is important in its own right, but as a citizen facing the hell that's going on in the world right now, do yourself a favor and learn the ones I outlined here. It will come in handy one day and perhaps even save yourself undue judgment. So, hypothetically speaking, what happens if you feel your Constitutional rights have been violated? United States law allows an individual who believes that his or her constitutional rights have been violated to bring a civil action against the government to recover the damages sustained as a result of that violation. This falls under what is known as "Tort Law". Quite interesting to learn about actually.

Yes, I went there. So, what is racism? Racism is defined as "prejudice, discrimination, or antagonism by an individual, community, or institution against a person or people on the basis of their membership in a particular racial or ethnic group, typically one that is a minority or marginalized." Now that we have a full understanding of what racism is, let me throw this question out there. Who is racist? I mean, if you look up the definition of a racist, it says "a person who is prejudiced against or antagonistic toward people on the basis of their membership in a particular racial or ethnic group, typically one that is a minority or marginalized." I feel like I'm talking in circles.

It's 2023. We have Black Lives Matter (BLM) as well as an entire nation of black people yelling at white people, calling them racist.

Black people can call each other "Nigga", and that's completely acceptable. White people cannot use that word as it's racist. Hmm. The definition of that word (as honestly, I don't even want to use it again) is "a contemptuous (worthless) term for a Black or dark-skinned person" and flagged "Offensive". Alright. I would agree with that term and meaning, as well as being flagged offensive. No argument here.

Now, I personally have heard black people calling white people "cracker". Hmm. The definition Cracker, or sometimes white cracker or cracka, is "a racial insult directed towards white people used especially with regard to poor rural whites in the Southern United States. Commonly a pejorative (Negative or disrespectful)." Now, if I call a black person the "N" word, I would get my ass beat and be called a racist. If a black person calls me a "Cracka", I may get offended if I'm the type of person to get offended, and that's it. Why is this? What's racist? What's not? Why is it acceptable for white people to be victims of insulting and derogatory language by blacks, but not the other way around? I asked this very question to a BLM representative and was told this, "This is not that hard of a concept. What white people fail to realize is that for many many years, black people were slaves to the white man. We [blacks] were whipped, beaten and forced to do physical labor while the white families lived in lavish houses and owned us. We have gained certain rights over time, yet, there is still very much a racial agenda by whites towards blacks as we're viewed as 'less than human'".

I was honestly taken back. It was highly disturbing and shocking to learn that there are STILL people in today's society that are very angry about history. I will be the first to say I firmly believe history is not pleasant. History is violent, unfair and gruesome in a lot of elements. There's no denying that. I will also say that Passed by Congress on January 31, 1865, and ratified on December 6, 1865, the 13th Amendment abolished slavery in the United States. This means that I, personally, NEVER owned any black people as slaves. My parents never did. Their parents never did, and their parents never did, and so on, until you reach the mid-1800's. During that time in my family tree, I cannot say. If they did, I feel ashamed, yet understand that during those times, that was accepted as normal, just as today, it's accepted that some people identify as a fucking cat who pisses in the sandbox at school. Whether we agree with it or not, society normalizes certain things and it becomes part of history; good, bad or otherwise.

So, racism. Why do we STILL have racism in today's society? I mean, we've had both white and black presidents of the United States, black and white athletes, millionaires, doctors, lawyers, janitors, etc. Even down to residential dwellings. Both whites and blacks live in apartments, trailer houses, single family homes, and mansions. So, why racism? I'm sure I will be depicted as having "white privilege" in saying this, but overall, in today's society, I see far more equality than racism, yet the word racism or "End Racism" is everywhere. Watch an NFL football game with 20,000 people in attendance, on the field by the endzones, it's painted, 'End Racism'; it's on their helmets too. What they call "peaceful protests" of BLM, many holding signs saying "End Racism".

Racism WILL end if they let it, but as long as the narrative of racism is alive and well, there's money to be made, so the more they push the phrase, "End racism" the more racism will be prevalent. Again, much of these falls under what I explained earlier about the war by division. Divide and conquer, right? Each day we are living on the verge of another civil war between race, religion and sexual identity. Can you imagine that war? Black against white against straight against trans against government against Christian against Muslim.... What a major clusterfuck. They're pushing this agenda to the point of reality. We just don't see it as the big picture still eludes us. We all need to come together as a human race and wake up. Take the red pill, so to speak.

Blind

One of the biggest headlines of our current time is the murder of George Floyd in Minnesota. When I say "George Floyd" I would bet you have at the very least heard that name before. So, what happened in the George Floyd incident? Mainstream media said that George Floyd was a black man who was profiled by Minnesota's white police officers and targeted. He was harassed, physically removed from his vehicle with force and suffocated on the street under the knee of the white officer. He was coined as stating, "I can't breathe" before he took his last breath. Awful. The police officers involved were all tried and convicted, and the streets of Minneapolis were destroyed, lit on fire, and looted. Chaos ensued and a portion of Minneapolis where George Floyd died was named, "George Floyd Square" where a mural was painted and peace was practiced. "End racism" was literally everywhere.

Now, there are always two sides to every story, right? I'm not in any way saying George Floyd deserved to die, deserved to be suffocated, or in any way saying what happened was 100% completely disgusting, however, George Floyd was not a saint. He was a convinced felon with a long wrap sheet. Let's expose this truth.

Born in Fayetteville, North Carolina, George Floyd grew up in Houston, Texas, playing football and basketball throughout high school and college. Between 1997 and 2005, he was convicted of eight crimes. He served four years in prison after accepting a plea bargain for a 2007 aggravated robbery in a home invasion. In looking at the public records of his criminal lifestyle, here's what can be proven as fact:

- 1997: Served for possession of cocaine
- 1998: Served 10 months for armed robbery
- 1998: Served again for robbery
- 2001: Failure to appear; listed as fugitive

- 2002: Served 8 months for cocaine possession
- 2003: Served time for trespassing
- 2004: Served 10 months for cocaine possession
- 2005: Served 10 months for cocaine possession
- 2007: Served 5 years for armed robbery of a pregnant woman in her home. Held a gun to her pregnant stomach and forcefully entered the home.

At the time of his death in Minneapolis, toxicology reports stated he was extremely high on fentanyl and methamphetamines, preparing to drive down a main street. Officers were called to the location of a convenience store where the clerk reported a "large black man" (never disclosed name of Floyd) used a counterfeit $20 bill to buy cigarettes, then ran outside to a vehicle when confronted. Officers responded as protocol and found Floyd in his vehicle, just sitting there. They approached the window and asked what he was doing and if he was "on anything". There was no response from Floyd, but the officer reported seeing a white foaming substance from the corners of Floyd's mouth. Officers asked Floyd to step out of the car as he was being placed under arrest for passing counterfeit currency. As they began to apply handcuffs to Floyd and escort him to the police squad car, Floyd stiffened up and used a "dead weight" technique to fall to the ground. He told officers he was not trying to resist, but did not want to get in the back of the squad car. Officers radioed for additional units to assist with Floyd. When on scene, the two additional officers assisted in the escort to the squad car where Floyd began stating he couldn't breathe.

Floyd was placed prone (face down) on the ground, with handcuffs still applied behind his back with officers in control of his feet, arms, shoulders and one officer kneeling on his face. He pleaded that he couldn't breathe, and even stated, "I'm about to die". During all of this, EMS was called for evaluation of Floyd while hundreds gathered with cell phones out, recording the incident. Civilians begging officers to get off Floyd as he couldn't breathe, and officers ignoring their pleas. EMS arrived and brought a lifeless Floyd to the ambulance and began chest compressions for revival but were unsuccessful.

The following weeks and months were mass catastrophes in Minnesota, Minneapolis and St. Paul specifically. Hundreds of protestors lit the city on fire. They rushed and burned down the third precinct (where these officers were from), vandalization and looting were constant and many lost their businesses. The mayor called a state of emergency and the National Guard was deployed to gain order. Together along with neighboring SWAT teams, destruction and violence ran around the clock to seek vengeance for George Floyd.

I live in Minnesota and I found myself needing to drive to and through downtown Minneapolis during this time. I will attest it felt and looked like a war zone. Camouflage wearing soldiers with automatic assault rifles standing in the streets with military vehicles everywhere was unsettling. It was a very eerie and odd feeling to know that we were always best known for "Minnesota nice" and now everywhere I looked was "Black Lives Matter" "Justice for George Floyd" and "Defund the Police" was spray painted on buildings, streets, police cars that had been previously burned to the ground. It was scary, to say the least.

So, now that I've explained the facts of the George Floyd case, I question WHY he has a mural painted on what was renamed, "George Floyd Square"? He's being revered as a hero; a martyr, or an "upstanding citizen". The New York Times even went so far as to write about Floyd's ancestry, stating, "We traced his ancestry back to a great-great-grandfather who was born and enslaved in North Carolina..."

Give me a break. We are glorifying a criminal, and apparently proud of it. The Prosecutor was quoted as saying, "His criminal history has no merit, because this is supposedly a country where, when you've served your sentence, you're now able to go rebuild your life, as what he was trying to do." So, he was trying to rebuild his life? By using counterfeit money for cigarettes. Seems legit.

His family then filed a lawsuit in the amount of $250 Million dollars for harassment, misappropriation, defamation and infliction of emotional distress. They ended up getting $27 million from the settlement. As of today, George Floyd himself is worth $5 million dollars.

Disgusting.

Social Status

Maybe you're a blue collar, physical labor person who works hard to provide for their family. Maybe you're a white-collar person in a management position who works long hours to put food on the table for your family. Maybe you're one of the elites in the realm of entertainment (Athlete, actor, entrepreneur). Regardless of who you are in the social status of life, we all play a part. We are all here for a common goal; to not only survive, but to thrive in what little time we have on this earth. What if this was all controlled by a higher power? I'm not talking about God, but the government. What if everything you did was controlled by the government? Let me explain. I spoke of this earlier, but in regards to the one world government, one of the things they're implementing is what's called a social credit system. What this means is that the social credit system primarily focuses on the financial trustworthiness of individual citizens.

One major focus is that of the "debt-dodger", a phrase which refers to those who can pay their debts but choose not to. A debt dodger blacklist is maintained by the Supreme People's Court. They determine whether you will be able to purchase items, food, goods or not depending on your trustworthiness. The more trustworthy you are, the higher your "credit score" is. The higher your score, the more perceived freedom you will have. I say "perceived" freedom because when this all comes full circle, EVERYTHING will be under their control and not yours anymore. It's all a game that needs to be played.

Let's break it down a little further. The social credit system will monitor EVERYTHING you do in your life. The purchase you make, depending on what the items are, will fall into a category and be given a score. The amount of money you spend on any given good will be categorized and given a score. Your daily interaction online (bank accounts, websites, social media, etc) will be categorized and given a score. All these and other scores will be collected and populated, giving you your social credit score. Example. Go to Facebook, and post the phrase, "I'm so proud to be an American". The next person posts, "America is destroying us". The positive message will be given a higher credit score than the lower one, PLUS, the lower one will be flagged as a threat to National Security for NSA follow up. Those who have a higher social credit score will have a much easier time getting a loan, making more money, being "allowed" to purchase entertainment tickets or access to events, whereas a lower credit score will prevent all of these, and perhaps even get you blacklisted until you're forced to change your behaviors.

It's all about regulation and control. Now, you may say that you will never allow the government to access your data, or download your finances, but let me ask you this. During the COVID pandemic, did you ever once get tested for the virus? Did you ever get that swab to the nose, or use your saliva for the test? What about watching or reading the percentages of positive vs negative COVID cases? How do you think they got those numbers? Everything is connected and pre-planned. Anyone who got swabbed inadvertently allowed the FDA/CDC "government" to collect your DNA sample. The DNA sample was then downloaded into the system and given a label. Disagree with any of this? Just simply look it up. It's able to be accessed by the public if the public wants to find it. The entire population's DNA has been downloaded to a main hub where it will stay until the microchip is enforced. All of this already is connected to the social credit score system that will be implemented in the very very near future.

For reference, feel free to look up the details on ESG (Environmental Social Governance). In February of 2022, Forbes.com published an article which read, "Environmental, social, and governance (ESG) metrics are a kind of social credit system designed to coerce businesses—and, by extension, individuals and all of society—to transform their daily practices.

Through a carrot-and-stick approach, investors and banks (and soon governments) use ESG to push businesses to change how they function, regardless of what the employees and customers of those businesses want. In many cases, however, corporate executives are all too willing to go along, because they want access to the cheap capital offered by investors and financial institutions.

The widespread adoption of ESG metrics, which is also commonly called "stakeholder capitalism"—is meant to radically alter how businesses and citizens are evaluated, expanding considerations beyond traditional economic metrics like profit, revenue, debt, customer satisfaction, and product development."

In an article published in April of 2022 in Reuters.com, an economic specialist wrote, "Unlike in China, our corporate shareholders still exhibit a need to thinly veil their dystopian plans, so they've decided to first roll out ESG scores as a tool for 'sustainable investing'. That is, they will first apply ESG scoring only to corporations to measure their compliance with 'climate', 'diversity', 'reputational', and corporate governancc requirements. This will presumably dictate the appeal of a company for 'ethical' investors. Of course, this is nothing more than a means of enforcing Democratic political dogma universally and a gigantic new scam for consultants who can improve ESG scores for a fee". ESG scores won't stay confined to public companies. They will expand out to privately held firms and individuals, with tax or credit worthiness penalties for anyone who doesn't pass woke brainwashing. It will become the primary means by which the globalist predator class maintains order and compels hypnotic compliance. They don't like what you say or do? Simple; No car loan, no mortgage, no passport, no plane ticket. Ironically, the timing couldn't be better. Almost everything you do is already captured on your phone, as I already mentioned, and the ability to track even more is just around the corner. Blockchain based digital identity and Central Bank Digital Currencies (CBDC) will soon provide a window into the finest details of your spending habits.

Tie your digital ID to your social media and even your opinions can be easily quantified. An AI generated social credit score will be unbelievably easy to create. There are already AI tools on the market that scan the news for mentions of your company and develop reputational scores based on what they find. Truth.

All this begs the question, "what will give you a bad ESG score?" There's no need to speculate for public corporations. The criteria is already being proudly broadcasted by the management consulting firms who will be some of the biggest beneficiaries of the new system. A few top factors include 'carbon footprint', resource use, board and employee 'diversity', executive pay, political lobbying and donations, the ESG standing of investment portfolios, and even the ESG scores of clients and suppliers.

That right, your ESG score can be docked simply because of who you associate with, as I mentioned in a previous chapter, we are losing our freedoms. So, what will this eventually mean for individuals? Probably like something inspired by a mixture of the book of Revelation and science fiction! You can certainly expect to be evaluated against your investment portfolio to start with. That will most likely expand out to how much you drive or fly, how much meat you eat, opinions you state or accounts you like on social media, how many minority owned businesses you do business with, your mRNA booster status, and the scores of your friends and family. But why stop there? With the magic of modern technology, what else could they possibly track?

Since the new fascist globo-state is a corporate inspired creature, we can anticipate the public being subjected to a whole slew of corporate HR style conformity tools.

Maybe your ESG score will drop because you've fallen behind on your mandatory weekly wokeness training or lacked enthusiasm in your latest required white privilege self-criticism submission. Or maybe you forgot to take your children to 'Drag Queen Story Hour' at the local library this week. Or maybe that co-worker with an unrequited crush on you feels particularly slighted one day and drops an anonymous tip that you've been tossing around racial slurs in the break room. None of these possibilities are really that wild or without precedent. The same controls are already largely in place through the private sector today, with less severe consequences, and participation in propaganda training sessions have been commonplace in many dystopian societies like Mao's China, Soviet Russia, Nazi Germany, and modern North Korea. Technology just makes more information about you available. It allows for a more perfect totalitarianism. I, personally, am far past ready to ditch EVERYTHING and go live off the grid with nature and avoid being manipulated or controlled any more.

If someone looked at you and said, "You're being watched 24/7/365, would you believe them? Would you be freaked out? You shouldn't be scared; however, you should believe them and pay attention to how you conduct yourself. Do you have a smartphone? Smart TV? Smart car? Do you know that smart is an acronym for Surveillance Monitoring Analyzing Reporting Technology? You ARE being watched and monitored already and have been since the birth of the smartphone.

Have you ever used voice-to-text on your phone, or how about asking Siri or Alexa something? You guessed it. All of that is collected and stored in *your* file; wherever that is in the cloud. In fact, in reading an interview with a former CIA agent, he opened up about the Artificial Intelligence of Alexa and Siri. He explained that there are algorithms that sift and sort various recordings and look for keywords that get flagged for review. There are agents that their sole job is to review transcripts of voice to (whatever) for threats or concerning language. That's just one element of all of this. Social media is amazingly intrusive. Facebook, Instagram, TikTok, Snapchat, LinkedIn, Twitter, Tumblr, and the list goes on. Everything you post, comment, like or insert (photo, video) is all recorded and monitored. Even when your device is powered off and, on the table, it DOES continue to monitor conversations and record them for download to your file. Have you ever had your phone turned off, or your TV turned off and had a conversation only to see ads for the item/good you were just talking about when you turn it back on? It happens. As I touched on in the previous chapter, you are always being watched, monitored and analyzed every minute of every day. Even things you wouldn't think are being logged and recorded are, such as what time you wake up in the morning, your real-time location 24/7/365, what phone calls you make, to who, how long they last, what text message you send to who and even what is said to what time you go to sleep, how long you sleep and the monitoring goes on and on and on...

Anything and everything you have on your phone is logged, analyzed and monitored, even any apps you have downloaded and/or are logged into. Even if you're not logged into the app, if you have an account, it's accessible. Take your financial institutional app. Do you have the ability to check your bank account on your phone? So do they. Spending monitoring Has been gathering data for some time so that when this next wave of Socialism gets placed into effect, you will already have a foundational social credit score.

One additional layer to this onion is the Restrict Act. See, the "Restrict Act of 2023" (S-686) which I found on www.Congress.gov was hidden within a myriad of other bills that are in the legislature as I write this. The language within the multi-page act DOES state some concerning language. Under subd. D, a line reads, "Any past, present, or future disparaging commentary", so once it's passed, anything you wrote anywhere on social media (or said in the "privacy" of your home if you even have Siri or Alexa) in the undefined past that is negative towards any governmental or political entity, they can use it to charge you with violating the terms of National Security. This was introduced to Congress on March 7, 2023.

Contact your local senators and express your desire to veto this bill; if it's not already too late.

What is "CERN"? Have you heard of it? CERN is the European Organization for Nuclear Research. Ok, so? Well, essentially, they spend millions researching molecules. See, all matter except dark matter is made of molecules, which are themselves made of atoms. Inside the atoms, there are electrons spinning around the nucleus. They're trying to see what the absolute smallest particle actually is; they're trying to recreate the big bang. Why am I sharing all this? Stick with me, I'll get there. CERN laboratories is located in **Geneva, Switzerland**. The logo of CERN is the word "CERN" surrounded by three rotating number 6's. Yes, 666. Hmm... Wait, there's more. In the book of Revelation 2: 12-13, it states, *"And TO THE ANGEL OF THE CHURCH IN *PERGAMOS* write; These things saith he which hath the sharp* *sword with two edges; I know thy works, and where thou dwellest, even where Satan's seat is: and thou holdest fast my name, and hast not denied my faith, even in those days wherein Antipas was my faithful martyr, who was slain among you where Satan dwelleth."*

Simply put; Antipas was killed where Satan lives.

So, where exactly was Antipas killed? Let me explain. During the reign of the Roman Emperor Nero, John the Apostle ordained Antipas as bishop of Pergamon, according to Christian tradition. Antipas was put to death during the reign of Nero (54-68), burned in a brazen bull-shaped altar at the Apollyon temple in Lyon/**Geneva Switzerland**, and buried in a nearby cemetery.

So Atipas was slain in what is modern day Geneva, Switzerland by being put in a bull shaped caldron of all things. So, by this, we learn that this is where Satan lives. Now let's think about some of the things that are headquartered in Geneva and it totally makes sense that this is where Satan truly would dwell here on Earth in the spiritual if not even the physical sense.

What's the deal with Geneva, Switzerland? Well, here's a list of entities whose headquarters are located in Geneva:

1. CERN particle accelerator

2.World Economic Forum Headquarters (remember Klaus Schwab?)

3. World Trade Organization

4. World Council of Churches

5. World Federation of United Nations

6. World Health Organization

7. World Meteorological Organization

8. International Lesbian, Gay, Bisexual, Trans and Intersex Association

9. GAVI (World vaccine alliance)

10. Lutheran World Federation

11. Internet Governance Forum

12. UN/USA embassy

In 2017, the world's largest and deepest railway tunnel was completed that connected the Swiss alps between the towns of Erstfeld in the north and Bodio in the south called the "Gotthard Base Tunnel", which was more than 7,500 feet deep and 35 miles long. Just a bit ago, I referenced the biblical location of where Satan resides on earth. Geneva. We've established that. The location of this tunnel is only a three-hour car drive to the tunnel. When the tunnel was officially opened, the opening ceremony, according to NBC news, was "satanic". Now, why in the world would a ceremony for a tunnel be deemed satanic? Let's look into this.

If you investigate this online, you will find endless video footage of the opening ceremony, which I will say, of all the things I've had to see in my life, this was the most disturbing. Among the attendees of the ceremony were an array of world leaders, celebrities, and elitists (very similar to the WEF gatherings). The first thing was, the tunnel was blessed by a priest, then over an hour of a choreographed display of haunting, dark, eerie sounds and music with hundreds dancing and removing their clothes, hanging by chains followed. Dancers dressed up like goats, and angels with the entire tunnel lit up with red lighting. The dancing became almost zombie-like and manic. Dancers became nude or nearly nude, showing compulsive type, almost trance-like moves. About nine minutes in, everyone begins worshiping a hairy, goat/human-like figure who is singing and speaking in gibberish. Evil, horror-like laughing can be heard in the background.

The rest you'll have to watch for yourself; it was far too disturbing for me to rehash. All for an opening ceremony for a tunnel.

Again, why all this for a railroad tunnel? Well, at this point, most answers are just theories. Many say due to the location and depth, this tunnel is the passageway to hades, or hell. Being that there is solid belief that the devil rules and resides in Geneva, it's a very convenient location to visit hell. Some say that as you get that deep that close to Geneva, evil spirits and demons overtake you and you lose all control; essentially Hell takes over. Reports dictate that while building the tunnel, more than 200 workers lost their lives. In October 2001, a

collision of two trucks created a fire in the tunnel, killing eleven and injuring many more, the smoke and gasses from the fires being the main cause of death. A blaze erupted within the tunnel during a commute including up to 40 cars and vans, most fused to a molten mass, were reported to be at the heart of the disaster zone. Officials said it could take days to establish the final death toll. These and many more oddities have happened and continue to occur in the Gotthard Tunnel, just outside Geneva, Switzerland. Some theories also include the use and research of CERN is to eventually actually open the portal to hell itself so it can be studied. According to top scientists at CERN, the ability to actually do this task is "surprisingly within reach".

Power Grid

Maybe you haven't been exposed to what a power grid is or how it all works. Being from the United States, I will solely speak on the US power grid.

A power grid is essentially the heart of our electric system. Meaning, it governs literally EVERYTHING that has to do with electricity in our country. From traffic lights to houses, buildings, hospitals to gas stations. With no power going to these places, there would be no way to pump gas to your vehicle as pumps are electric. There would be no way to heat or cool your homes, or cook, as everything requires electricity. Even gas stoves require some element of electricity. Even companies would crash due to no internet! Let's take a hospital for example, take away all electricity from hospitals. No lights, no emergency medical equipment operation, no heat, no air, no security, nothing. You see, eliminating a power grid would bring our entire country back to the stone age.

The United States Department of Homeland Security has recently (2023) disclosed new details about the extent to which Russia has infiltrated "critical infrastructure" like American power plants, water facilities and gas pipelines. So, basically, everything that I just stated "could" happen if the process of the power grid crashes has already been started by Russia's Vladimir Putin. Between the state and federal level, top officials have been discussing the security of such an "attack", which they've come to find is a catch 22. There really is no way to fully secure our power grids without spending an astronomical amount which is simply not fathomable.

Even as far back as 2018, the Cybersecurity & Infrastructure Security Agency (CISA.gov) was investigating Russia's presence in cybersecurity malware detection. According to the CISA, a memorandum posted stated, "This joint Technical Alert (TA) is the result of analytic efforts between the Department of Homeland Security (DHS) and the Federal Bureau of Investigation (FBI). This alert provides information on Russian government actions targeting U.S. Government entities as well as organizations in the energy, nuclear, commercial facilities, water, aviation, and critical manufacturing sectors. It also contains indicators of compromise (IOCs) and technical details on the tactics, techniques, and procedures (TTPs) used by Russian government cyber actors on compromised victim networks. DHS and FBI produced this alert to educate network defenders to enhance their ability to identify and reduce exposure to malicious activity."

This is described as a multi-stage intrusion campaign by Russian government cyber actors who targeted small commercial facilities' networks where they staged malware, conducted spear phishing, and gained remote access into energy sector networks. After obtaining access, the Russian government cyber actors conducted network reconnaissance, moved laterally, and collected information pertaining to Industrial Control Systems.

This was back in 2018. Five years prior to me writing this. So, let me ask you. What advances has Russia made in this operation? It would be safe to say, probably more than any of us really know.

So, how many power grids are there in the United States? One? Two? Several? How they're set up is like this. There are only THREE main power grids; Eastern, Western and Texan power grids. Those three branch out into nine main sub stations. Those nine branch out into others which branch out into others. It's like how oceans are connected to lakes, lakes to streams, streams to ponds and so on. If someone wanted to completely destroy us as a country and cause 100% chaos nationwide, they only have to take out three main plants. Like dominos, the rest would fall almost immediately and within seconds we would all be living like our primitive ancestors.

One of the most concerning concepts of all this is that to find the actual location of any of these three power grids, all you have to do is a simple Google search.

According to Forbes.com, "Protecting critical infrastructure, and especially the U.S. Energy Grid is certainly a topic that keeps the U.S. Department of Homeland Security (DHS), The U.S. Department of Energy (DOE), The U.S. Department of Defense (DOD), and U.S. intelligence community planners up at night.
 The threats can be from cybersecurity attacks (by countries, criminal gangs, or hacktivists), from physical attacks by terrorists (domestic or foreign) and vandals on utilities or power plants, or from an Electronic Magnetic Pulse (EMP) generated from a geomagnetic solar flare, or from a terrorist short range nuclear missile exploded in the atmosphere."

As of 2023, Russia and China are the only two countries that physically possess the ability to deploy an EMP through nuclear weaponry. What I found somewhat comical, yet supportive, was that when you go and do a search asking, "How to survive an EMP attack", the list of prepper and survivalist websites and forums is palpable. Surviving an EMP attack would require a combination of primitive skills and self-sufficiency. Having enough food, water, and medical supplies will be critical for survival. Without those, there really is no chance. Having said that, with the idea of an EMP being deployed, it won't harm us physically as humans as the electricity spike would go into our bodies and through our legs to the ground. That's it. It would only pose a danger to those with any internal electronic equipment such as a pacemaker or something similar.

Just think of the overall big picture and how everything is connected. With an electromagnetic pulse, it would shut down ALL things electric and/or electronic. No gas for cars; no cars, as the pulse would destroy the electronic system. No cars/trucks mean no transportation of food. No food in grocery stores, means YOU have to feed yourself however you can. This and more are the mindset of preppers worldwide. They spend months, even years, or a lifetime stocking up on canned and boxed goods along with bottled water and first aid materials along with firearms and ammunition. They are prepared to protect their own families in the event of a worldwide or nationwide catastrophe. They study human behavior and understand that when things get right down to starvation, people will fight or kill for food. Preppers plan to ward off those who are coming for food. Undoubtedly, when/if this were to happen (which according to every governmental entity that has a letter abbreviation says it's inevitable) only the strong will survive. Movies like Mad Max, Legion, and other Apocalyptic films are not too far from being accurate.

Why are more and more people growing their own food? Because many (not all) farmers are using toxic chemicals to kill weeds and enhance the production of soy, corn, rice, potatoes, tomatoes, canola oil, papaya, beets, and the list goes on. Did you know up to 90% of soybeans have been genetically modified (GM)?!?! Genetically modified corn is listed as "not safe for human consumption". This includes corn products (beer, salad dressing, flour, margarine, corn syrup) Implanted genes are being traits in rice to increase the amounts of Vitamin A levels. Unless it's listed as "Organic Potato", you can guarantee it's been genetically modified in some fashion, and listed as "not safe for human consumption".

As far back as 1994, tomatoes were GM where an enzyme was deactivated that caused rot; therefore, keeping the tomato "fresher longer", but in turn creators began seeing it was carcinogenic. Canola oil, used in processed food, Chios, crackers, cereals, snack bars, frozen foods, canned soups, bread and oil blends is one of the most heavily modified crops, all to make it easier for weed control at harvesting. Aspartame. Read regular and diet soda.

Aspartame is an artificial sweetener. Aspartame is categorized according to the FDA, as 200 times more potent than natural sugar! Aspartame is made from two bacteria that make an acid then modified to boost production. Ongoing concerns of cancer-causing agents within aspartame. Do yourself a favor. Next time you're shopping for food, READ THE LABELS. Stick to the outside of the store and avoid the middle rows. Look at the ingredients. Stick to items that have the LEAST amount of ingredients. Those will be closest to natural. Easy rule of thumb;
Natural = healthy

Healthy= won't kill ya.

Be safe. Be smart. Be educated.

Another hidden in plain sight element is Bioengineered food ingredients. In some cases, they're talking about the Soy Lecithin. Soy Lecithin is essentially formulated in a lab and although the FDA says it's not harmful at all, any bioengineered ingredient can introduce novel organisms into our bodies that can read havoc. For example: toxicity, allergic reactions, antibiotic resistance, immuno-suppression, cancers, loss of nutritional value... So why do they bioengineer food ingredients?

Taste. That's it. So, the question is, do you trust the FDA? The FDA being the same entity that publicly proclaimed the COVID 19 vaccine was safe? I wouldn't.

End of Times

This topic is something I've been fascinated by for some time, so naturally, I've spent quite some time really studying it, learning about it and accurately separating fact from fiction; or rumors.

Amongst the myriad of events and biblical red flags that are happening and continue to happen in our world, the question remains, are we in the end of times? Will the world come to an end soon? Well, that question has been asked for hundreds, if not thousands of years by people watching their own times, and finding parallels to biblical events. Matthew 24:36 states, "Concerning that day and hour no one knows, not even the angels of heaven, nor the Son, but the Father only." Meaning only God truly knows when our last day will be. Having said that, there are several events that have taken place in the last year or two and are happening right now that have never happened in the history of the world, that were prophesied.

For example, in Job 12:7 it states, "But ask the animals, and they will teach you, or the birds in the sky, and they will tell you." Referring to the coming of Christ and what to watch for when He is about to return. The crow is a spiritual symbol of change, transformation, and

Death. Right now, as I write this, Israel is coming up on their 70th week; also known as "70 Weeks of Daniel". Six acts take place within these 70 weeks:

- Finish the transgression.
- Make an end to sins.
- Make reconciliation (atonement) for iniquity.
- Bring in everlasting righteousness.
- Seal up vision and prophecy.
- Anoint the "Most Holy."

Jesus has fulfilled the first three already, and Satan is trying to stop the other three from happening. This is explained in Daniel 9:24-27. In the book of Ezekiel 38-39, it explains that in the end times, Israel needs to fall and be destroyed to prepare for the coming and anointing of the False Messiah, which needs to happen before the Antichrist is announced. Again, I completely understand how this all sound like a science fiction novel. It did to me at first also until I began really watching what's going on around the globe.

So, going back to Job 12:7, on April 30, 2023, in Israel, witnesses took video of a single crow landing on top of an Israeli flag pole, and literally pecking at it until the flag fell to the ground. When it fell, the crow flew off. Now, reading these words, I can appreciate that one would have a hard time believing this, but this short video clip gained well over 106,000 views worldwide and has thousands preparing for the next sign of the times. If you would like to view the video, if it's still available, here is the link: https://youtube.com/shorts/ZilIK7TyQlO?feature=share

In looking at the false prophet and antichrist angle, I'm not at all saying I know for certainty who they will be, however, what I have found is a man named Yehuda Rav Shlomo Yehuda from Israel. He's 33 years old (same age as Jesus was when he was crucified). Yehuda came out of nowhere and now is in the spotlight in Israel. Thousands claim he knows the entire Bible cover to cover, has actively healed several people (Blind to see, crippled to walk) and speaks of peace and love. Calling himself "the Messiah". Sound familiar? Revelation 13:11 talks about a false prophet being like a lamb, likable, and humble. We are not to be fooled as he is a predator.

Matthew 7:15 states, "Beware of false prophet as they come to you in sheep's clothing but inwardly, they are ravenous wolves".

Now, don't be confused, this is for sure NOT the Antichrist, but this false prophet has been sent out before the exposure of the antichrist. This false prophet will gain the trust of the world, and direct people to worship the Antichrist. This is all to prepare for the One World Religion where Satan will be the focus of power and worship.

Alright; one question for you. Do you ever watch World News? Not the gimmicky crap, but actual facts of what's going on across the globe? I never did, BUT I really have been, BECAUSE a lot of what's going on today has been prophesied in the Bible! I get super excited when it happens!

If you go online anywhere, I'm sure you may have heard something about us living in the end times. Well, without sounding like a paranoid schizophrenic, we are. Fact. The question still remains, "When is the ACTUAL last day?" We may soon find out. See, from reading the Bible, and studying theology and world events, it is prophesied that essentially Russia will cause the third world war, which will signal the end of times. Here's what I've gathered over the last few years....

Israel, the Holy Land, has, for ages, been the focus of torment by other countries. There will come a day where Israel will be in battle (in some form) with Arabic countries. It may even be now. Tensions will escalate, and a powerful leader will publicly announce a peace treaty between the Arab people and the Israeli people. At the time things will seem amazing, however at this time of the announcement, many will not understand that this powerful leader will actually BE the Antichrist, and the peace will be a false sense of peace. As the Arab people are within this peace treaty (that will only last 7 years), they are also joining an alliance with Vladimir Putin's Russian military. Russia will join forces with Kazakhstan, Tajikistan, Uzbekistan, Kyrgyzstan, Turkmenistan, Afghanistan, and Pakistan (which were all part of Persia in Biblical times). Within 7 years, this alliance 8000 times larger than Israel will, as the Bible states, "Cover the people like a cloud". Or essentially obliterate the entire country of Israel in a matter of 6 days.

This will be considered around the world as "World War 3". After this occurs, the largest earthquake the world has ever seen will take place with the epicenter right in Israel. It will be so massive; it will not be able to be measured on the Richter's Scale. It will be so massive, that the entire earth will be affected and mass chaos will follow worldwide.   While all this is happening in the roughly 7 years and 6 days, Jesus and His army of Angels, Archangels, Principalities and even Virtues will be getting ready for His Second Coming, where Jesus Himself will walk this earth once again, for the last time.

I am hoping I will be able to visit the Holy Land before it's destroyed. Now, I don't know about you, but I am absolutely excited with just the thought of watching the news and watching this all unfold.   What an amazing time to be alive!

Closing

I understand I've thrown a lot at you in this somewhat small book, but the contents are both highly intense and factual. I do not follow a certain political party, simply because I am a follower of God and Jesus Christ. That's where my values and morals lie.

I also understand that the times we're living in with the One World (fill-in-the-blank), pride, monitoring and controlling, along with the normalizing public nudity and sex in front of all ages along with the major tensions that are rising between races, social statuses and religions are perhaps similar to times that have occurred in past generations and/or centuries. Many scholars and theologians have made tremendous similarities of today's times to that of the times of Noah and Sodom & Gomorrah. If you know, or recall, those times sin was suffocating the world with evil and that's the time where God told Noah to build the arc, then flooded the entire planet to rid the world of evil and sin. As the old saying goes, "History repeats itself". We are living in very similar times.

In the times of Noah, God gave a vision to all of a rainbow, as a promise to never flood the world again. This rainbow has been hijacked by evil and used to mock God to use it for the pride of their wicked ways. This time, God will not flood the earth. This time it will be much different, and I pray that I am around to witness the unspeakable display of the war of Armageddon.

Anything in this book is searchable and able to be verified if you think anything is far-fetched or made up. I warn you though, if anything in this book made you think I was crazy, or way off base, before you look for yourself, ask yourself one question. By researching yourself, you are then essentially taking the red pill. There is no turning back. If you are in disbelief about this book, learning for yourself what I've said here will change your entire life, and you will not be able to unsee it.

Many people are woke. Some are awake. There are really only two options here. If you choose to take the red pill and look into these things yourself, it will be hard to believe, but you will have an awakening. I'm just trying to prepare you for what I've already gone through. It's pretty amazing, honestly. Nothing has ever been the same for me since then. I truly hope I was able to open your eyes to the truth and in turn, I hope you share the truth with others to keep them safe and alive.

May God Bless you for reading this and opening your heart, eyes and mind to be awake to the Clown world Matrix.